ELOTE
MEXICAN CORN

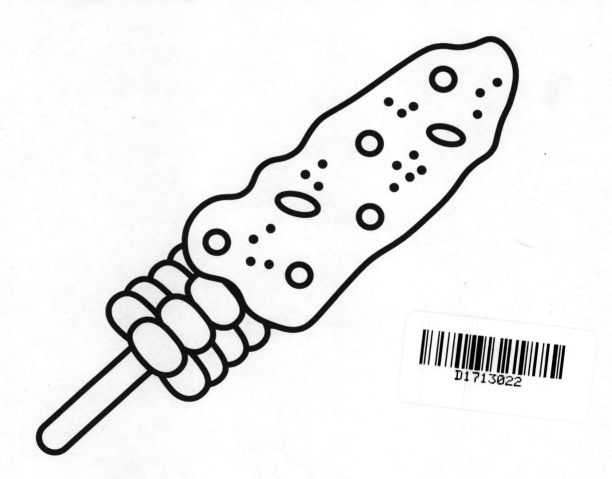

MEXICAN TREATS
COLORING BOOK
70+
DESIGNS

CHURROS

DE LA ROSA MAZAPAN

CONCHA

TAJÍN

TAJÍN

JARRITOS

BURRITO

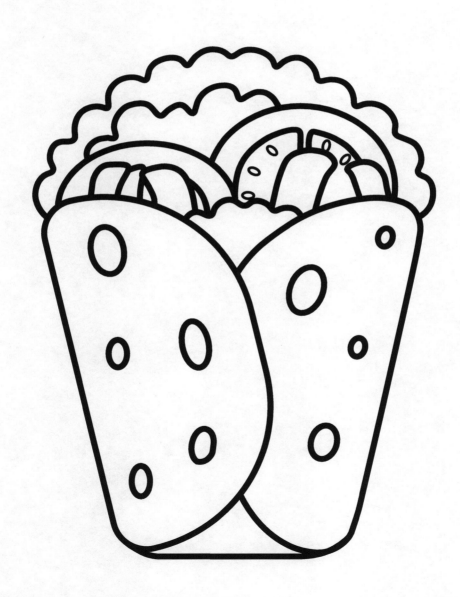

ROSCA DE REYES

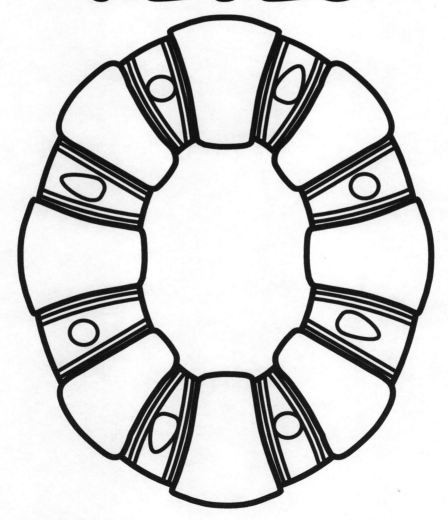

NACHOS

MEXICAN BAÑUELOS

PELON PELO RICO

GANSITOS

VERO MANGO

MEXICAN JUICE

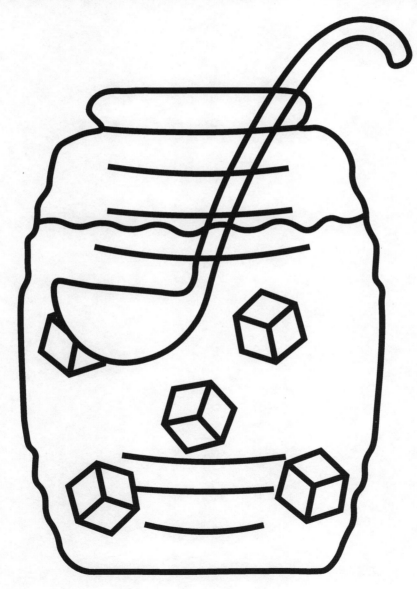

MEXICAN COCONUT FLAG

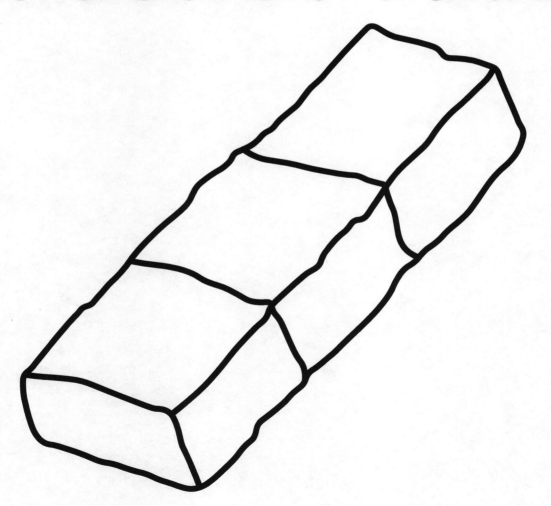

MANTECADAS

CACAHUATES JAPONES

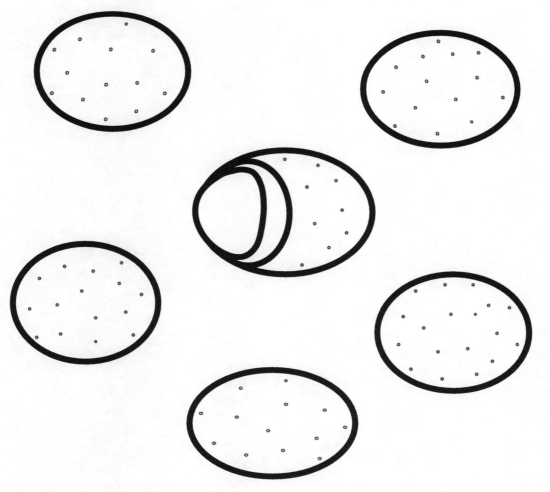

CHILI MANGO

BANDERILLAS

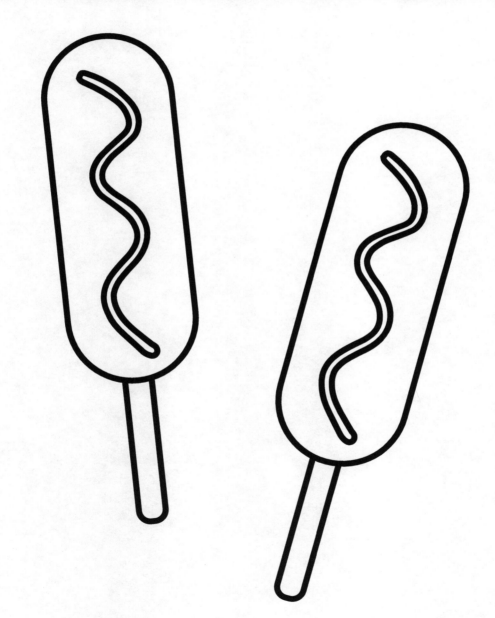

BANDERILLAS

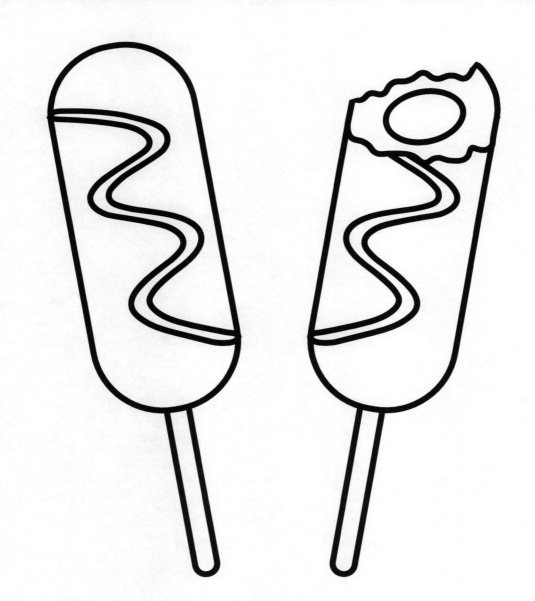

LUCAS

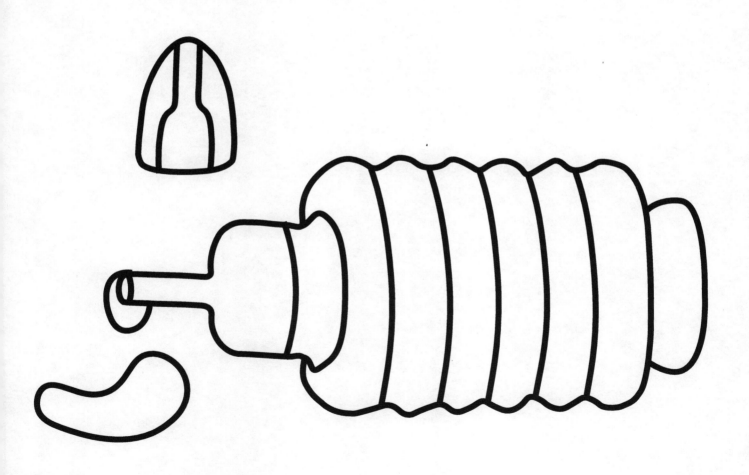

CINNAMON APPLE EMPANADAS

REBANADITAS
WATERMELON
LOLLIPOPS

GALLETAS DE GRAGEAS

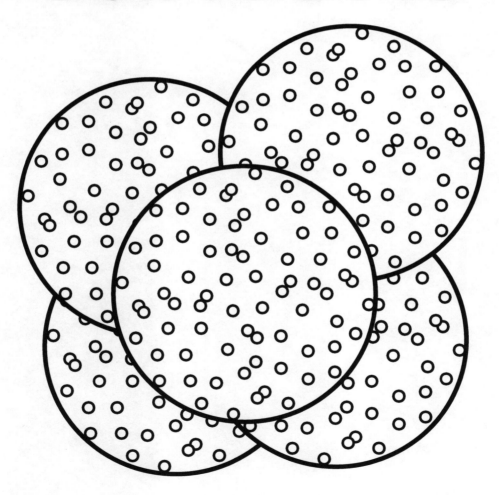

BUBULUBU

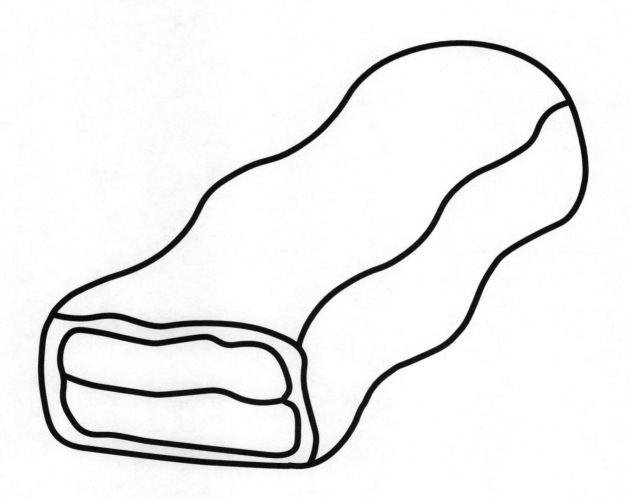

DUVALÍN

LOLLIPOPS

MEXICO DRINK IN A BAG

CROISSANT

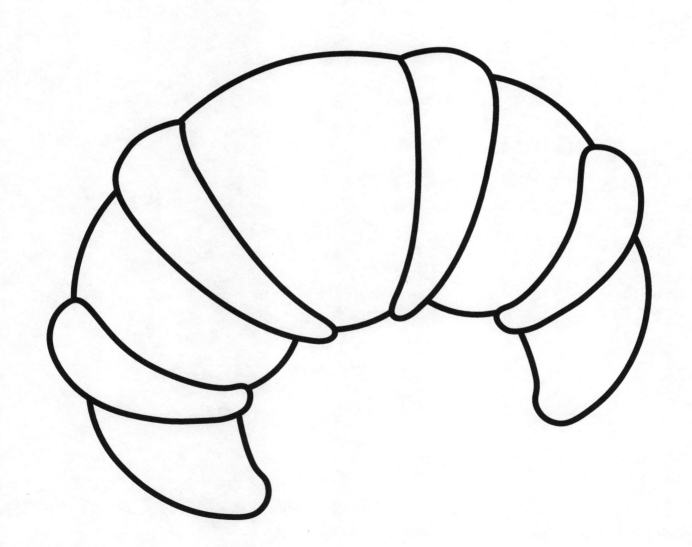

SATAY

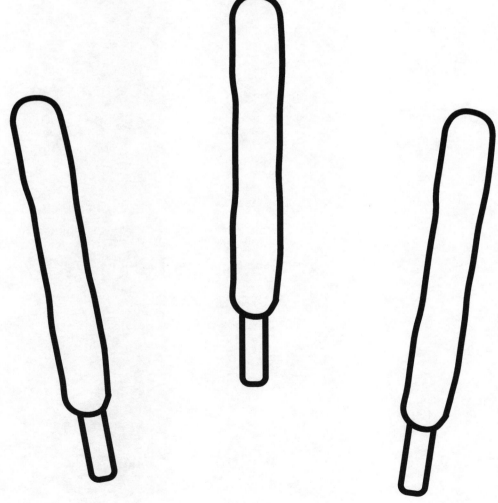

PALETAS DE FRESA

SPONCH COOKIES

GELATINA DE ROMPOPE

POLVORON TREBOL

ELOTE
MEXICAN CORN

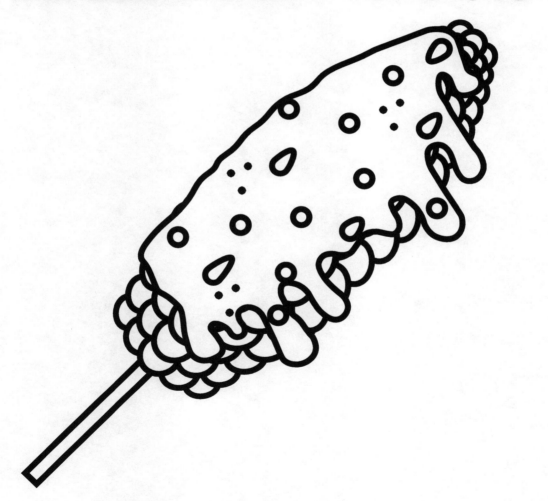

CHILI MANGO

MEXICAN CHURROS

NACHOS

NACHOS

BURRITO

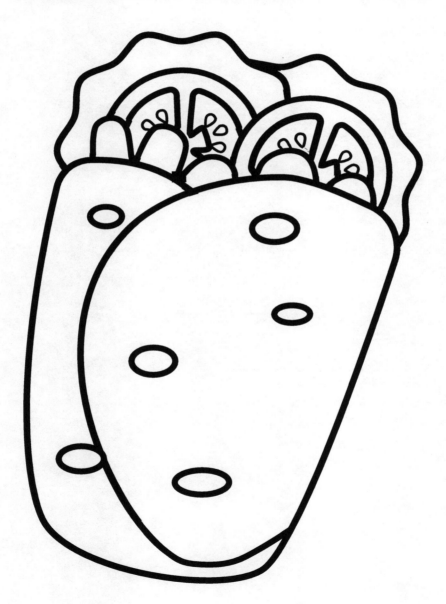

PAN DE MUERTO

MEXICAN BAÑUELOS

TAMALE

SOPES

LOLLIPOPS

PALETA
PAYASO

FLAUTAS

CANTARITOS COCKTAIL

ENCHILADA

CHAMPURRADO

PELON PELO RICO

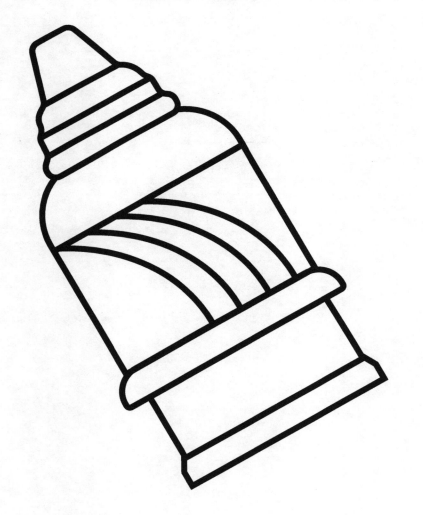

CHILAQUILE

CARNITAS

ARROZ CON LECHE

CONCHAS

CONCHA

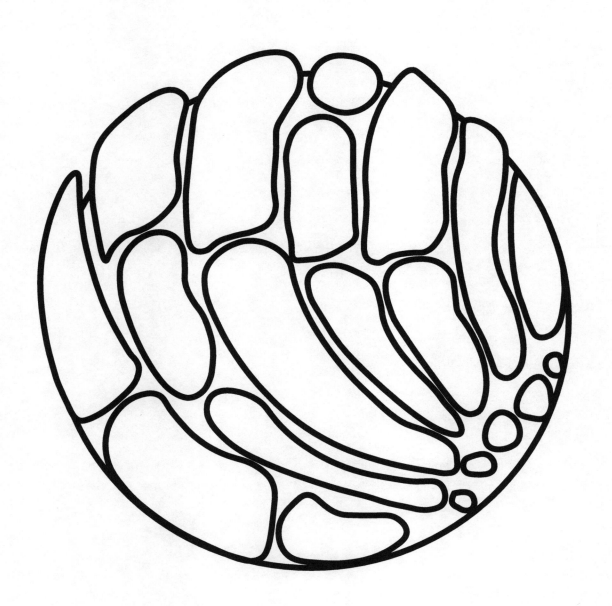

AGUACHILE

HOT SAUCE

CHILI SAUCE

CAJETA COFFEE

QUESADILLAS

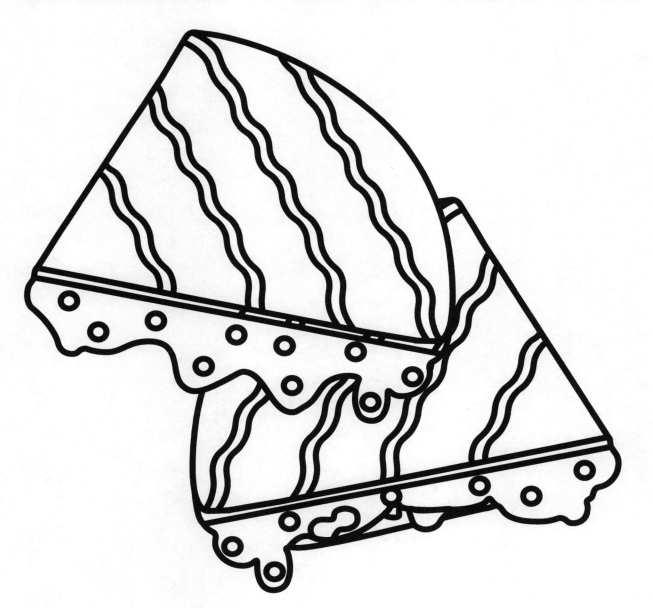

TACO

TACO

CHURROS

BOLILLOS

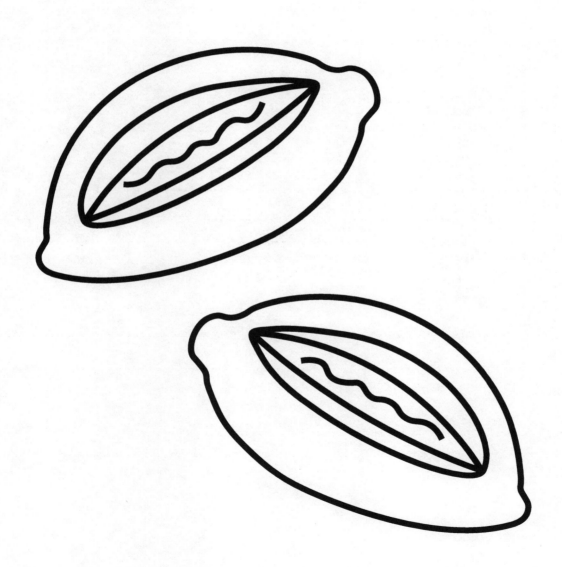

CINNAMON APPLE EMPANADAS

NIÑO ENVUELTO

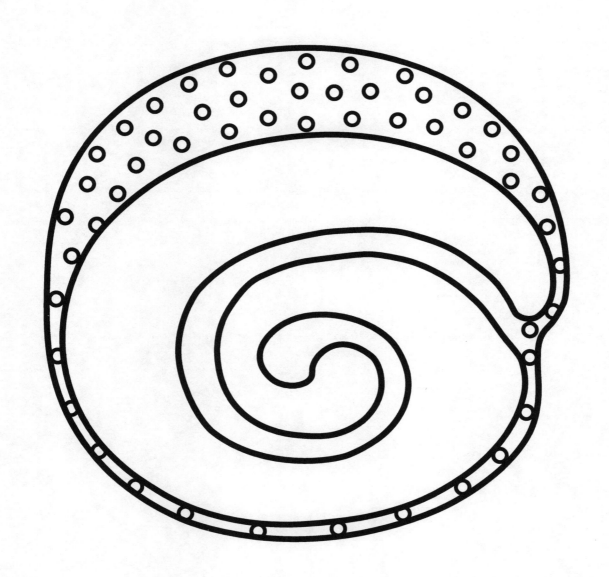

LUCAS MUECAS CHAMOY

LUCAS MUECAS CHAMOY

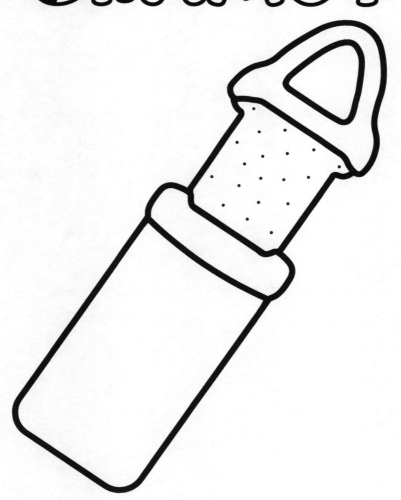

TEQUEÑOS

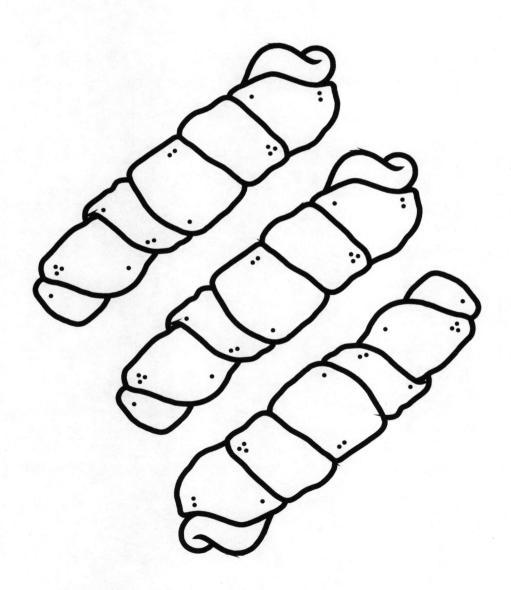

PAMONHA

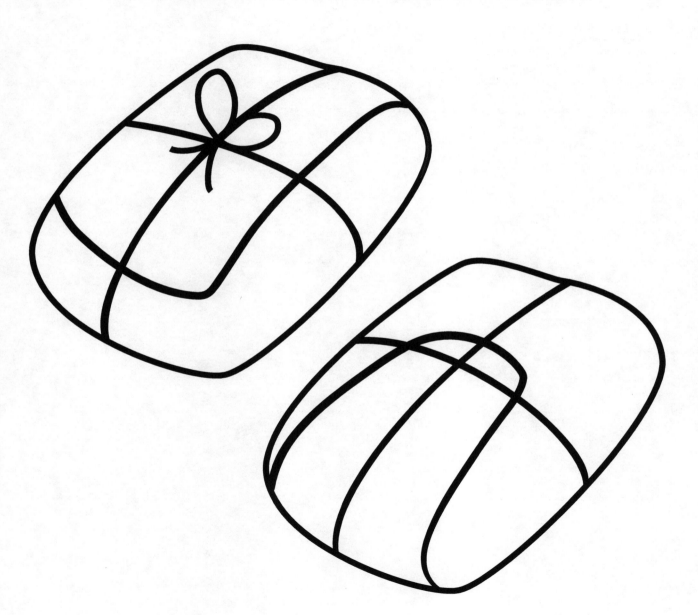

CHAMPURRADO

MOLCAJETE

Made in the USA
Monee, IL
25 September 2024

66612484R00083